Contents

KU-679-538

All about winter

The cold, frosty days of winter can be a great time to get outside if you put on warm clothes. This book is full of art projects and things to make and do outside in winter. Have fun!

When is winter?

Winter happens at different times of the year in different parts of the world. In the northern half of the world, winter lasts from December until March (or until the temperature rises and we see the signs of spring in nature). In the southern half, it lasts from July to August.

Winter is the season between autumn and spring. It has the shortest days and longest nights of all the seasons. As the days grow shorter, the temperature drops and it can be cold and wet. Overnight frosts, sleet and snow are all possible in winter. In the morning cars are often covered with white frost. Puddles, ponds and lakes can turn to ice.

It is important to wear warm clothes when you go outside in winter. Keep away from frozen ponds, but have fun cracking the ice on puddles.

The Outdoor Art Room
Winter

Rita Storey

W
FRANKLIN WATTS
LONDON • SYDNEY

Franklin Watts
Published in paperback in Great Britain in 2018 by The Watts Publishing Group

Copyright © The Watts Publishing Group 2015

All rights reserved.

Series editor: Sarah Peutrill
Art direction: Peter Scoulding
Series designed and created for Franklin Watts by Storeybooks
rita@storeybooks.co.uk
Designer: Rita Storey
Editor: Sarah Ridley
Photography: Tudor Photography, Banbury
Cover images: Tudor Photography, Banbury
Cover design: Cathryn Gilbert

Every attempt has been made to clear copyright. Should there be any
inadvertent omission please apply to the publisher for rectification.

Dewey number 745.5
ISBN 978 1 4451 4371 2
Library ebook ISBN 978 1 4451 3971 5

A CIP catalogue record for this book is available
from the British Library.

Printed in China

MIX
Paper from
responsible sources
FSC® C104740
FSC
www.fsc.org

Franklin Watts
An imprint of
Hachette Children's Group
Part of The Watts Publishing Group
Carmelite House
50 Victoria Embankment
London EC4Y 0DZ

An Hachette UK Company
www.hachette.co.uk

www.franklinwatts.co.uk

Before you start

Some of the projects in this book require scissors or a sewing needle
and the handling of ice and peanuts. When using these things
we would recommend that children are supervised by
a responsible adult.

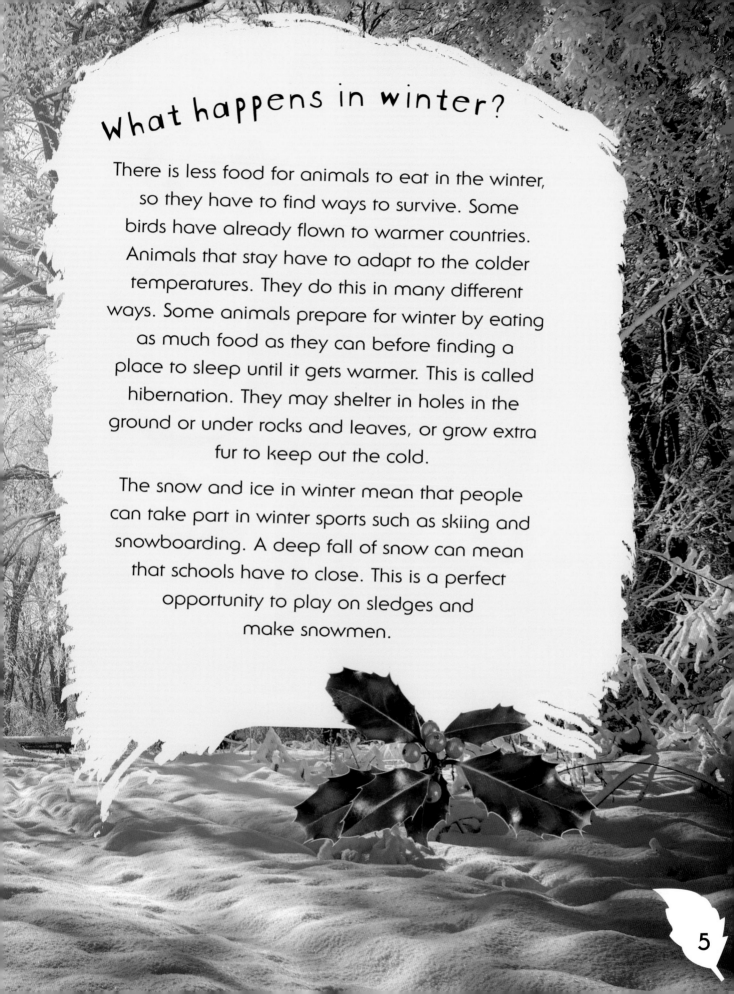

What happens in winter?

There is less food for animals to eat in the winter, so they have to find ways to survive. Some birds have already flown to warmer countries. Animals that stay have to adapt to the colder temperatures. They do this in many different ways. Some animals prepare for winter by eating as much food as they can before finding a place to sleep until it gets warmer. This is called hibernation. They may shelter in holes in the ground or under rocks and leaves, or grow extra fur to keep out the cold.

The snow and ice in winter mean that people can take part in winter sports such as skiing and snowboarding. A deep fall of snow can mean that schools have to close. This is a perfect opportunity to play on sledges and make snowmen.

Snow scene

Winter brings snow to many parts of the world. Even if you do not have any snow, you can use fake snow to build a snow scene.

You will need:

* 500g bicarbonate of soda
* large mixing bowl
* shaving foam
* fork
* plastic tray
* model house (optional)
* 2 red beads
* 3 green beads
* 5 small black beads
* tiny twigs

Trees in winter

Many trees are bare in winter. Their leaves fell off during the autumn months. Autumn and winter storms sometimes make twigs break off the trees and fall to the ground. Collect some to use in art projects.

1 Tip the bicarbonate of soda into the bowl. Add a 3-second squirt of shaving foam.

2 Stir with a fork until the mixture has a snowy texture.

3 Put three-quarters of the mixture into a tray. If you have a model house place it on the fake snow.

4 Add another 3-second squirt of shaving foam and mix it into the remaining mixture.

To make the snowman

 Take half of the remaining fake snow and roll it into three balls. Stack them one on top of the other in the tray. Push the beads and twigs into the balls of snow, as shown in the picture.

To make the reindeer

 Roll the rest of the fake snow into two balls. Stack one on top of the other. Push the beads and twigs into the balls as shown in the picture on the right.

Good news! This fake snow does not melt, but it does dry out after a few days.

Glowstick lanterns

Cheer up a dark winter evening with these colourful glowstick lanterns.

You will need:

* clear glass bottles and jars
* squares of blue and red tissue paper, measuring 2cm x 2cm
* squares of purple tissue paper, measuring 1cm x 1cm
* PVA glue
* paintbrush
* glitter glue
* glowsticks (3 or 4 per bottle or jar)

1 Paint PVA glue onto some blue squares of tissue paper. Stick them around the outside of a bottle so that one corner of each square points upwards.

2 Paint PVA glue onto some red squares. Stick them around the bottle above the blue squares so that one corner of each square points upwards.

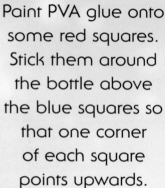

3 Repeat step 2 with the purple squares. Stick them above the red squares, as shown. Draw a line of glitter glue around each square. Leave to dry.

4 Follow steps 1–3 to decorate more bottles or jars. You could use different coloured paper.

5 When it gets dark, bend the glowsticks so that they begin to glow.

6 Share the glowsticks among the jars and bottles.

Be patient. Do not bend the glowsticks until it is completely dark.

Light in winter

In winter the days are short and the nights are long. The lengths of the days and nights vary from country to country, depending on how far north they are. At the North Pole, there are 11 weeks of complete darkness in mid-winter.

Decorate a tree for the birds 1

These pretty bird treats look great on the bare branches of a tree in winter. Watch to see how many different types of bird visit your tree.

1 Pour the bird seed into the mixing bowl. Ask an adult to melt the lard in the saucepan. Leave it to cool for 5 minutes. Stir it into the seeds.

You will need:

* 50gm bird seed
* medium-sized mixing bowl
* 50gm lard
* saucepan
* wooden spoon
* star biscuit cutter
* aluminium foil
* pieces of raffia 20cm in length

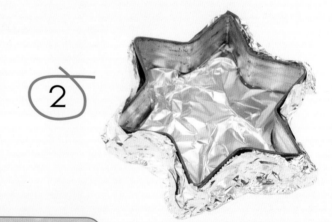

2 Wrap foil around the bottom and sides of the biscuit cutter, as shown.

Birds in winter

Birds have several layers of fluffy feathers to trap heat and keep them warm in cold weather. Finding food can be more of a problem in winter, which is why it is a good idea to feed garden birds.

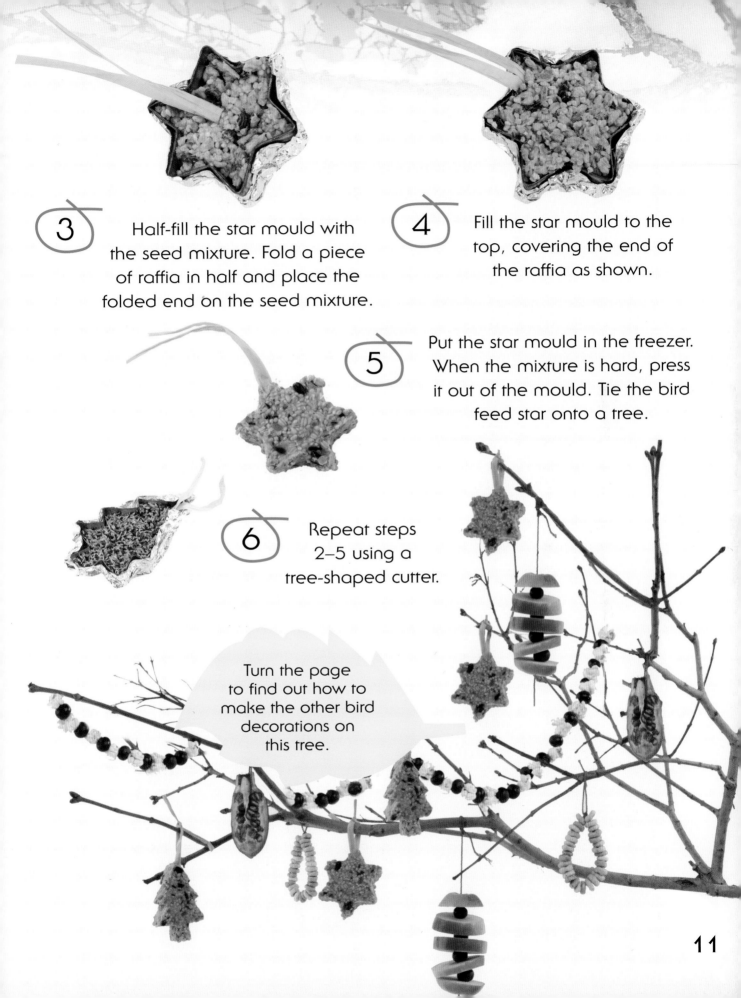

3 Half-fill the star mould with the seed mixture. Fold a piece of raffia in half and place the folded end on the seed mixture.

4 Fill the star mould to the top, covering the end of the raffia as shown.

5 Put the star mould in the freezer. When the mixture is hard, press it out of the mould. Tie the bird feed star onto a tree.

6 Repeat steps 2–5 using a tree-shaped cutter.

Turn the page to find out how to make the other bird decorations on this tree.

Decorate a tree for the birds 2

These bird treats will attract lots of birds to a bare winter branch. Some birds feed on the ground, so you could put some treats on the ground for them to enjoy as well.

To make the pomegranate decoration

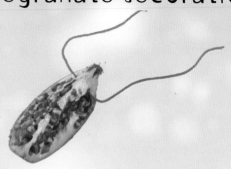

Ask an adult to thread the needle with thin string. Push the needle through the top of each pomegranate slice. Tie the decoration onto a twig. Repeat to make more like this.

You will need:
(for the pomegranate decorations)
* pomegranate, cut into slices
* embroidery needle
* thin string, cut into 20cm lengths

(for the cereal loops decoration)
* cereal loops
* thin string, cut into 30cm lengths

To make the cereal loops decoration

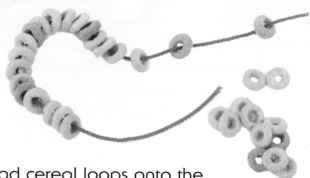

Thread cereal loops onto the string. Tie the ends of the string together. Hang your cereal loop on a twig in a sheltered place to avoid the loops going soggy. Repeat to make more.

To make the apple and blueberry decoration

You will need:

(for the apple decoration)
* an apple, sliced across the middle
* 4 blueberries
* embroidery needle
* thin string, cut into 15cm lengths

(for the popcorn garland)
* plain 'popped' popcorn
* blueberries
* embroidery needle
* long piece of thread, 50cm in length

Tie a knot in the string. Ask an adult to thread a needle onto the other end and then push it through an apple slice and a blueberry. Repeat to create several layers. Tie the decoration onto a branch.

To make the popcorn garland

Ask an adult to thread the needle with thin string. Push the needle through a piece of plain 'popped' popcorn and then through a blueberry. Repeat until your garland is long enough.

Birds need fresh water to drink in winter. Put a shallow bowl of water in your garden. Remember to change it regularly, especially in cold weather.

Giant spider

Some garden spiders shelter in our homes over the winter, while others make webs inside hollow logs or in sheds. This spider is looking for a big meal before he finds a place to spend the winter.

You will need:

* black or dark purple paint and a paintbrush
* polystyrene balls, 1 x 10cm across and 1 x 7cm across – you can buy these in a craft shop
* 2 cocktail sticks
* 2 googly eyes
* PVA glue and spreader
* 4 black pipe cleaners
* scissors
* ruler

1 Paint the polystyrene balls black or dark purple.

2 Push a cocktail stick into one of the polystyrene balls.

3 Push the second polystyrene ball onto the other end of the cocktail stick until the two balls meet.

4 Glue on the googly eyes.

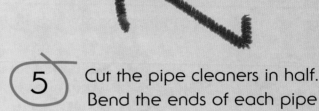

5 Cut the pipe cleaners in half. Bend the ends of each pipe cleaner, as shown above.

6 Use a cocktail stick to make four holes in a row on each side of the spider's body, about 1cm apart.

7 Push the end of each pipe cleaner into the eight holes in the polystyrene ball.

Turn the page to make a huge web for your spider, so that he can catch a giant fly.

Multicoloured web

Spiders spin beautiful webs from silk thread to catch insects. Look outdoors for webs sparkling with frost in early winter.

 1 Tie the ends of the length of orange raffia together to make a loop.

You will need:

* 1 x 15cm length of orange raffia
* 6 x 25cm lengths of raffia in different colours
* 4 long lengths of red, green, pink and yellow raffia
* scissors

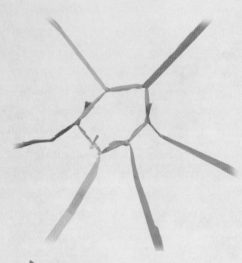

2 Knot the six 25-cm lengths of raffia onto the orange loop.

 3 Tie the ends of each length of raffia onto the branches of a tree, as shown in the photo on the left. Trim the ends.

4 Tie the end of the long length of red raffia onto one of the 25cm strings, about 5cm from the orange loop at the centre. Wrap the raffia around the next string, keeping it tight, but not too tight. Wrap it around the next string.

5 Repeat all the way around and tie the end of the raffia in a knot.

6 Repeat steps 4 and 5 with the green, pink and yellow strings of raffia.

Look who has moved in! It is the giant spider from pages 14–15 trying to catch a fly!

17

Ice bowl

To make this bowl outside you need very cold weather. As the ice bowl starts to melt, birds can eat the seeds and nuts trapped in the ice.

You will need:
* 200ml water
* large plastic bowl
* medium-sized bowl
* seeds, berries, leaves, nuts, cereal
* ruler

(1)

Pour 200ml of water into the large bowl. Put the medium-sized bowl inside the large bowl.

(2)

Arrange the seeds, berries, leaves, nuts and cereal in the space between the two bowls.

All about ice

When water gets very cold it stops being a runny liquid and turns into a solid block called ice. To turn water into ice the temperature has to be below freezing (0^0C).

3. Top up the water between the two bowls until the water level is about 3cm from the top of the smaller bowl. Put the bowl outside overnight.

4. Pour some warm water into the medium-sized bowl to loosen it. Take it out and place it to one side. Now dip the large bowl in warm water briefly so that you can slide it off your ice bowl.

5. Place the finished ice bowl where the birds will find it outdoors. As the ice melts, it will also create a drinking bowl for the birds.

If the temperature outside is not low enough to turn the water to solid ice, put the bowls into the freezer for two hours.

Stone art

In winter there are very few colourful flowers in the garden. These painted stones will add a splash of colour until the flowers bloom again in spring.

1 Paint the stones different colours. Leave to dry.

You will need:
* small, flat stones
* red, orange, yellow, blue and purple acrylic craft paint
* paintbrush

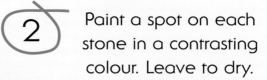

2 Paint a spot on each stone in a contrasting colour. Leave to dry.

3 Finish by painting a coloured dot in the centre of each stone. Leave to dry.

④ Lay out your stones on a hard surface. Start in the centre, placing the red stones in a spiral shape.

⑤ Continue with the spiral shape, using the orange stones.

⑥ Now place the yellow, blue and purple stones to complete the spiral.

There are lots of other patterns you can make with these colourful stones. Change the pattern every now and again.

Rainbow ice sculptures

Freeze water in an old rubber glove to make an ice sculpture. You could make another shape using a jelly mould or a balloon.

You will need:

* old rubber glove (without holes)
* 2 long knitting needles
* ruler
* plastic bucket
* measuring jug * water
* green, yellow and blue food colouring
* scissors

This activity will only work when it is VERY cold. If it is not cold enough, use a plastic cup instead of a rubber glove and freeze the sculpture in the freezer.

1 Ask an adult's permission before you use the rubber glove. Ask them to push the knitting needles right through the cuff of the rubber glove, leaving a 2cm-gap beween the two needles.

2 Balance the knitting needles over the plastic bucket, as shown.

3 Fill the jug with water and add some green food colouring.

Fold back the cuff of the rubber glove. Pour the coloured water into the glove until the water is up to the top of the fingers. Leave everything outside overnight to freeze hard.
Repeat step 4 with yellow water.
Repeat step 4 with blue water.

 Snip off the glove. Stand the ice hand up somewhere where you can see it as it melts slowly.

Ice hands will begin to melt as soon as the temperature rises above freezing (0°C).

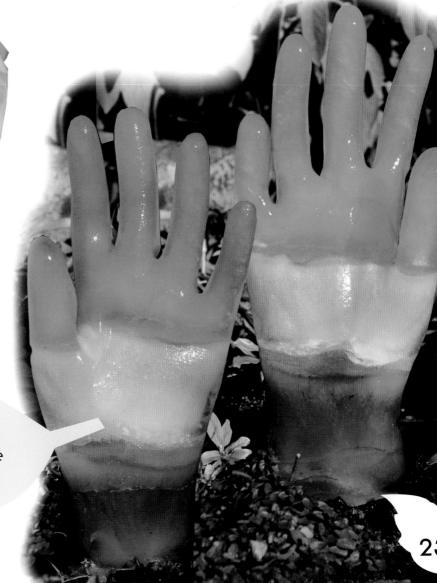

Snow animals

If you are lucky enough to have some snow in the winter, why not make a snow caterpillar or a snow bear instead of a snowman?

You will need:

(for the caterpillar)
* snow * 3 twigs
* 2 seeds

(for the snow bear)
* snow
* 3 small round stones or pebbles
* 7 small oval stones or pebbles

To make the snow caterpillar

1. Make nine snowballs of the same size.

2. Place the snowballs in a wiggly line.

3. Finish off the caterpillar by adding two twig antennae, two seed eyes and a twig mouth.

Snow

Snowflakes are made when tiny water droplets freeze in the sky to form ice crystals. When enough crystals have joined together, they become heavy and fall as snowflakes.

To make the snow bear

1. Make a large snowball and a slightly smaller snowball. Place the smaller one on top.

2. Make seven small snowballs. Place four of them on the bottom snowball to look like arms and legs. Put two on either side of the top snowball to look like ears. Put one onto the middle of the top snowball to look like a muzzle.

3. Use the small round stones to give the bear eyes and a nose. Use the oval stones to add a mouth and three claws on each paw.

Giant snowflake

Flakes of snow are small and delicate, but lots of them can build up in winter to make a thick covering of sparkly snow. This big snowflake will sparkle too as it hangs on a door.

You will need:

* 3 large red lollysticks
* strong glue and spreader
* 6 small coloured lollysticks
* PVA glue
* glitter
* 7 sparkly stars
* string
* adhesive tack

If you cannot buy coloured lolly sticks, paint some wooden ones before you begin.

1. Use strong glue to glue two large red lollysticks together to form a cross.

2. Glue the third red lollystick on top to form a six-sided star shape.

3. Glue three small lolly sticks across the ends of the large sticks, about 1cm from the end.

4. Repeat to add three more sticks. Glue the end of the last stick underneath the red lollystick, as shown.

Glue the last small stick under the red lollystick

Spread some PVA glue onto the sticks and sprinkle it with glitter. Shake off the surplus.

Glue on a star where the red lollysticks cross over each other.

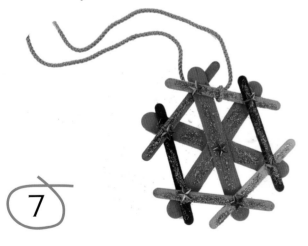

Tie the string to the snowflake and knot the ends together to form a loop. Hang the snowflake from a door, using adhesive tack.

Snowflakes

Snowflakes all have six points or sides. If you look at a snowflake through a strong magnifying glass you will see a beautiful pattern of ice crystals arranged in a hexagonal pattern. Every snowflake is slightly different.

Ice suncatchers

In very cold weather it is fun to make ice suncatchers that will sparkle in the winter sunlight.

1 Fill the plastic lid with water.

You will need:

* plastic lid
* water
* sequins
* confetti stars
* glitter
* piece of raffia, 20cm long
* blue and yellow food colouring

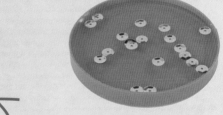

2 Sprinkle a few sequins on top.

3 Add some confetti stars.

4 Sprinkle a little glitter on top.

5 Fold the raffia in half. Lay the folded end in the water. Add one drop of blue food colouring.

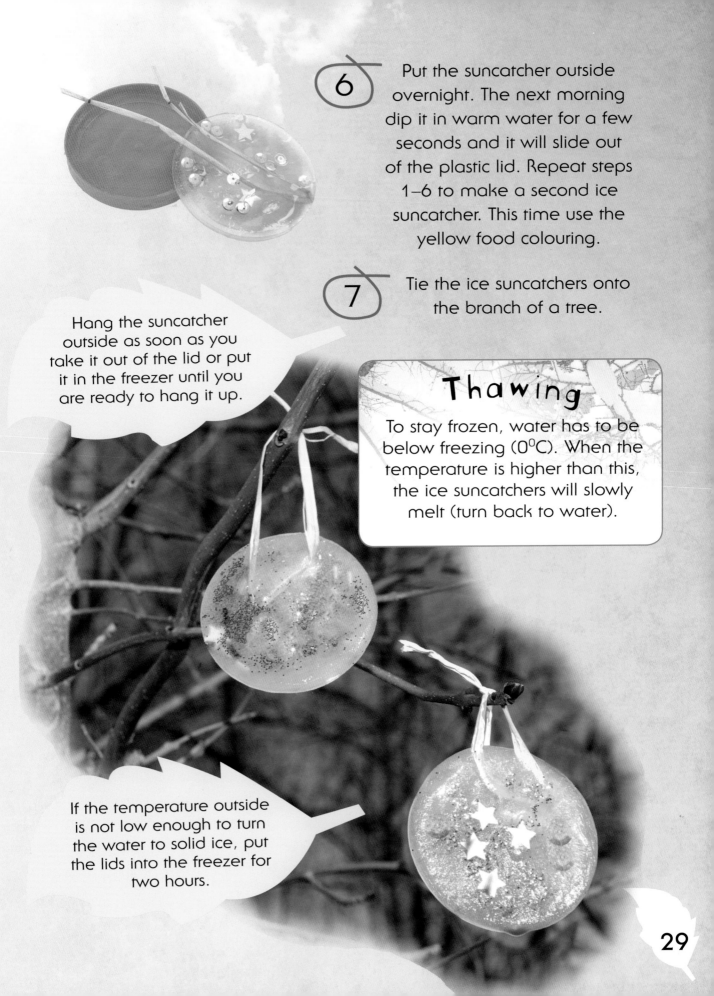

6 Put the suncatcher outside overnight. The next morning dip it in warm water for a few seconds and it will slide out of the plastic lid. Repeat steps 1–6 to make a second ice suncatcher. This time use the yellow food colouring.

7 Tie the ice suncatchers onto the branch of a tree.

Hang the suncatcher outside as soon as you take it out of the lid or put it in the freezer until you are ready to hang it up.

Thawing

To stay frozen, water has to be below freezing ($0^{0}C$). When the temperature is higher than this, the ice suncatchers will slowly melt (turn back to water).

If the temperature outside is not low enough to turn the water to solid ice, put the lids into the freezer for two hours.

Winter words

adapt change or find ways to suit new surroundings

antennae pair of thread-like projections found on the head of insects

droplet tiny drop of water or another liquid

frost frozen dew or water vapour

hexagonal having six sides and six angles

hibernation when animals go into a deep sleep to survive the winter

ice frozen water – its solid state; water freezes when it reaches temperatures below $0^{0}C$

ice crystal a small piece of ice with many even sides

lard pig fat that has been processed for use in cooking

magnifying glass a round piece of glass with a handle that magnifies objects, making them appear bigger than they really are

seed the part of a plant that grows into a new plant

snowflake tiny flake of snow

spider's web a network of fine silk threads that are made inside a spider's body and woven into a web to catch insects

temperature how hot or cold something is

thaw when a substance that was frozen warms up it thaws, becoming softer or liquid

Find out more

www.dltk-holidays.com/winter/
Lots of great winter-themed crafts and activities.

www.bbc.co.uk/nature/adaptations/Hibernation
The BBC Nature website with film clips about hibernation.

http://www.woodlandtrust.org.uk/naturedetectives/
Activities, games and ideas for winter, selected by the Woodland Trust.

Note to parents and teachers: every effort has been made by the Publishers to ensure that these websites are suitable for children, that they are of the highest educational value, and that they contain no inappropriate or offensive material. However, because of the nature of the Internet, it is impossible to guarantee that the contents of these sites will not be altered. We strongly advise that Internet access is supervised by a responsible adult.

Index